Legends of Rock

U2

Changing the World Through Rock 'n' Roll

by Jennifer L. Huston

Consultant:
Meredith Rutledge-Borger,
Associate Curator
Rock and Roll Hall of Fame & Museum
Cleveland, Ohio

CAPSTONE PRESS
a capstone imprint

Edge Books are published by Capstone Press,
1710 Roe Crest Drive, North Mankato, Minnesota 56003
www.capstonepub.com

Library of Congress Cataloging-in-Publication
Huston, Jennifer L.
   U2 : changing the world through rock 'n' roll / by Jennifer
L. Huston.
       pages cm.–(Edge. Legends of rock)
   Includes bibliographical references and index
   Summary: "Describes the rise to fame and the lasting impact
of the band U2"–Provided by publisher.
   ISBN 978-1-4914-1818-5 (library binding)
   ISBN 978-1-4914-1823-9 (ebook pdf)
   1. U2 (Musical group)–Juvenile literature 2. Rock musicians–
Juvenile literature I. Title. ML3930.U2H87 2015
782.42166092'2–dc23 [B]   2014023797

Editorial Credits
Mandy Robbins, editor; Tracy Davies-McCabe, designer; Eric
Gohl, media researcher; Gene Bentdahl, production specialist

Quotation Sources
p. 6, Hot Press Yearbook, 1980, p. 7,8, U2 by U2, 2006, p. 51; p.
12, Rolling Stone magazine, March 14, 1985; p 17, From the Sky
Down, 2011; p 19, Lyrics from "I'll Go Crazy If I Don't Go Crazy
Tonight" from No Line on the Horizon; p. 20, U2 by U2, 2006,
p. 266; p. 29, U2 by U2, 2006, p. 345.

Photo Credits
Alamy: Andrew Fox, 18 (top); AP Photo: Timm Schamberger,
cover; Corbis: Martyn Goddard, 7, Sygma/Andrew Murray,
18 (bottom), Getty Images: Dave Hogan, 17, Redferns/Clayton
Call, 11, Redferns/David Corio, 9, Redferns/Eamonn McCabe, 18
(middle), Redferns/Ebet Roberts, 21, Redferns/Hayley Madden,
22, Redferns/MAI/Lex van Rossen, 12-13, Redferns/Mick Hutson,
19, Redferns/Rob Verhorst, 5; Glow Images: Africa 24 Media/
Riccardo Gangale, 23; Newscom: EPA/Andrzej Grygiel, 26-27,
Everett Collection, 25, Mirrorpix/Rosenbaum, 15, ZUMA Press/
Nancy Kaszerman, 28

Design Elements
Shutterstock

Printed in the United States of America in
Stevens Point, Wisconsin.
092014   008479WZS15

Table of Contents

Introduction: I Will Follow **6**

Chapter 1
Stories for Boys **6**

Chapter 2
Elevation **10**

Chapter 3
We're One, But We're Not the Same **16**

Chapter 4
Into the Heart **22**

Glossary **30**

Read More **31**

Internet Sites **31**

Index **32**

I Will Follow

You've camped outside the stadium all day. You can hardly wait for your favorite band, U2, to take the stage. Once inside the stadium, you stake out some prime real estate on the floor. For the next few hours, you'll be jumping up and down and screaming your lungs out.

The crowd roars as the first notes of "City of Blinding Lights" ring out. Chills run up and down your spine. Slowly, one by one, the band members take their places on the stage. Bono appears last from behind a cloud of smoke. The crowd goes wild.

If You Dream then Dream Out Loud

U2 is a musical powerhouse that sells out stadiums across the globe. The band has sold millions of albums. They've won every musical award there is, including more **Grammy Awards** than any other rock band.

But U2 wasn't always the "greatest band in the world" as they've often been called. They started out as four teens from Ireland who could barely play their instruments. They've come a long way since their shaky start in the late 1970s.

Grammy Award: an award given at an annual music awards celebration that honors the year's best music

A concert in Las Vegas, Nevada, kicks off U2's PopMart tour in 1997.

U2's Top 10 Songs

1. "With or Without You"
2. "I Still Haven't Found What I'm Looking For"
3. "Desire"
4. "Mysterious Ways"
5. "One"
6. "Discothèque"
7. "Where the Streets Have No Name"
8. "Angel of Harlem"
9. "Hold Me, Thrill Me, Kiss Me, Kill Me"
10. "Beautiful Day"

*Note: Songs are ranked by chart position on *Billboard*'s Hot 100.

Stories for Boys

In 1976 drummer Larry Mullen Jr. was 14 years old. He pinned a note on his school bulletin board hoping to start a band. On September 25 several boys showed up at the Mullen house for auditions. They set up in the kitchen and showed off their musical skills.

"The fact that [none of us] could play or sing was but an obstacle to overcome."

—Bono

Not long after that first rehearsal, Feedback was born. The band consisted of lead singer Bono, guitarist The Edge, bassist Adam Clayton, and Larry Mullen Jr. The Edge's older brother, Dick, who played guitar, was also briefly a member. Feedback practiced and began to improve. The band members started writing their own songs and matured as a group. They also changed their name to the Hype.

After Dick left the band, the remaining members decided a name change was needed, so they became U2. Their first show as U2 was a talent contest in the Irish town of Limerick in 1978. The top prize was £500 (about $950) and a chance to record a single for CBS Records. The boys of U2 thought they had no chance of winning. But they did!

"[when] we walked on that stage ... I just started to levitate ... Everything changed for me, because now I knew what I wanted to do for the rest of my life." —Bono remembering his first gig

U2 band members in their London home, 1979

What's in a Name?

Bono and The Edge were teenagers when they earned their nicknames. Originally, Bono's nickname was Bono Vox, which means "good voice" in Latin. It came from a sign on a hearing aid store in Dublin. The Edge's nickname describes the strong angles of his face, as well as his sharp mind and way of looking at things.

Invisible

After the exciting victory in Limerick, Bono had plans for U2 to become the greatest band in the world. He may have been on to something, but it didn't happen overnight. When opening for a punk band later that year, an angry crowd spit at Bono. They threw lit cigarettes at the band. Despite such setbacks, U2 gradually built up a following of loyal fans.

In 1979 U2 made a record with CBS as promised. But the record companies weren't impressed. Eventually Island Records, a struggling independent label, took a chance on them.

It seemed U2 had what it took to make it big in the music business. Their manager believed in them. They had a growing following of fans in Ireland who believed in them. But most importantly, they believed in themselves. It was time to conquer the world.

"Before we could play, before we could write songs, before we could perform, we believed in ourselves as a band." —The Edge

U2 performing at Cork Country
Club in Ireland, 1980

Backstage Pass:

Bono

Real Name: Paul Hewson
Born: May 10, 1960, in Dublin, Ireland
Role: lead singer, songwriter,
harmonica and backup
guitar player
What he brings to the group:
Bono is not a trained musician.
But he shines as the front man
of the group. He has a talent
for engaging the audience and
connecting with them.

9

2

Elεvation

U2 signed with Island Records in March 1980. Their first album, *Boy*, was released that October. Fans were impressed by the band's melodic yet gritty sound. In December 1980 U2 played a handful of shows during their first trip to the United States. By the end of the tour, they had a growing American fan base.

In the fall of 1981, U2 released their second album, *October*. Many of the songs on the album are about God and spirituality. At the time, Bono, Larry, and The Edge became involved with a religious group. For a while they weren't sure they could maintain their religious beliefs and be in a rock band at the same time. They eventually decided they could.

With their third album, *War*, Bono took the lyrics in an entirely different direction. The most popular songs on the album—"New Year's Day" and "Sunday Bloody Sunday"—were inspired by political events. "New Year's Day" was written to support a social movement in Poland against the Soviet Union. With Larry's military-style drumming, "Sunday Bloody Sunday" is a protest song inspired by the political and religious troubles in Northern Ireland.

U2 Trivia

The song "Tomorrow" from *October* is about the death of Bono's mother. She died when he was 14. Bono and Larry both lost their mothers when they were teenagers. Bono says joining the band restored his self-confidence, which had been lacking since his mother's death.

The Edge and Bono at a concert in San Francisco, California, 1981

Backstage Pass:
· ·

The Edge

Real Name: David Evans

Born: August 8, 1961, in London, England (The Edge moved to Ireland when he was a baby.)

Role: lead guitar player, keyboard player, backup vocals, songwriter

What he brings to the group:
The Edge is completely self-taught. Over the years he has created a distinct, gritty sound that is uniquely his own. His ability to create new sounds helps U2 maintain its position in the music industry.

After their fourth album, *The Unforgettable Fire*, U2 started to gain worldwide recognition. Rock critics began taking notice. In 1985 they performed at Live Aid, a concert to raise money for victims of **famine** in Ethiopia. This event became a major turning point in the band's career. More than 1 billion people watched U2 steal the show when Bono jumped into the crowd and danced with a fan. His ability to connect with fans caused the band's popularity to skyrocket. That same year, *Rolling Stone* magazine named U2 its "Band of the '80s."

U2 took their time making their fifth album, and it paid off. The band released *The Joshua Tree* in 1987. The album won four Grammy Awards, including Album of the Year. U2 also scored its first two Number One songs on *Billboard* charts in the United States.

In 1987 *Time* magazine declared U2 "Rock's Hottest Ticket." The four Irishmen were now selling out stadiums around the world. As Bono had predicted back in the late 1970s, U2 had become the greatest band in the world.

" ... [F]or a growing number of rock-and-roll fans, U2 have become the band that matters most, maybe even the only band that matters."

Rolling Stone magazine, March 14, 1985

famine: a serious shortage of food resulting in widespread hunger and death

Bono captivates a packed arena of fans at a concert in the Netherlands, 1987.

In 1988 U2 released its sixth album, *Rattle and Hum*, which reached Number One on the U.S. and British music charts. A rockumentary film of the same name hit theaters around the same time. The movie gave viewers a sneak peek into life on the road with the world's biggest band.

By the end of the 1980s, U2 was exhausted and burnt out physically, emotionally, and musically. The members felt the need to take some time off to rejuvenate. At a show in Dublin in December 1989, Bono shocked the crowd with an announcement: "This is just the end of something for U2 … It's no big deal. We have to go away and just dream it all up again." After that the band took some time off. When they reunited in Berlin in late 1990, they took the opportunity to reinvent their image. But what followed nearly put an end to U2.

Backstage Pass:

Larry Mullen Jr.

Born: October 31, 1961, in Dublin, Ireland
Role: drummer
What he brings to the group: Larry started taking drum lessons at age 9, but he quickly lost interest in learning the basics. He learned to play rock music by playing along to records. His lack of traditional training makes his style completely unique.

Backstage Pass:

Adam Clayton

Born: March 13, 1960, in Chinnor, England (Adam moved to Ireland at age 5.)
Role: bass guitar, briefly manager
What he brings to the group: When Adam joined the group he owned a bass but couldn't play it. He learned to play along the way. Over the years Adam has settled into his role, contributing strong, supportive bass lines to the rhythm section without overpowering it.

The Dalton Brothers

A few times during the Joshua Tree tour, U2 came on stage in disguise and performed as an opening act. Dressed in wigs and western clothing, they called themselves the Dalton Brothers. In a southern accent, Bono took on the **persona** of Alton Dalton. He told the audience, "We play two kinds of music—country and western." Most fans were fooled, and some even booed them and told them to get off the stage!

THE EMPIRE The First 100 Years

rockumentary: a nonfiction movie or TV program about a rock band

rhythm: a regular beat in music, poetry, or dance

persona: a personality or character that someone projects to an audience that is not in line with his or her true self

We're One, But We're Not the Same

3

In October 1990 the members of U2 arrived in Berlin, Germany, to work on their next album. Larry and Adam wanted to stick with the kind of songs that had brought them success in the past. But The Edge and Bono wanted to switch gears and experiment with electronic dance music. Because of these creative differences, their recording sessions were going nowhere. The band members were frustrated and getting on each other's nerves.

But then something magical happened. The Edge was experimenting with a couple different chords. Producer Daniel Lanois suggested playing both of them at the same time. So The Edge played one chord while Adam played the other. Bono started tossing around some lyrics, and just like that, the song "One" was born. Soon after that, the album fell into place. In November 1991 *Achtung Baby* was released. It remains one of U2's most popular albums, earning a Grammy for Best Rock Album.

chord: a combination of musical notes played at the same time "we'd been going through this hard time, and nothing seemed to be going right. suddenly we were presented with this gift. it just kind of arrived."

— The Edge, referring to the song "One"

Backstage Pass:

Paul McGuinness

Born: June 17, 1951, Rinteln, Germany
Role: manager from 1978-2013
What he brought to the group: Paul McGuinness was the manager and unofficial "fifth member" of U2. He helped them get a record deal with Island Records when no one else would sign them.

In February 1992 U2 hit the road to promote *Achtung Baby* with the over-the-top Zoo TV tour. The tour poked fun at the excess of rock 'n' roll. Behind the stage dozens of TVs flashed random words, commercials, and live pictures of the audience. Cars dangled from the ceiling. Bono also adopted several off-the-wall personas during the Zoo TV tour. During a break in the tour, U2 recorded the *Zooropa* album. When the tour resumed, they added the new songs to the set list.

The Many Looks of Bono

Bono likes to have fun with his appearance. As "The Fly," Bono was decked out in shiny, black leather and big sunglasses. He strutted around on stage portraying the typical rock star. "Mirrorball Man" wore a silver suit and cowboy hat. "MacPhisto" was an old, washed-up pop star. For this character Bono wore a gold metallic suit with his face painted white and red horns on top of his head. While in character Bono often called the White House and asked to speak to then-president George H.W. Bush. He never got through. But while U2 was hosting a radio call-in show in 1992, presidential candidate Bill Clinton called them.

"The right to appear ridiculous is something I hold dear."

Bono

U2 Trivia

On average every day of the Zoo TV tour cost about $125,000 whether there was a show or not.

U2 experimented even further with their next album, *Pop*. But a dark cloud seemed to hang over the band during the making of the album. Larry was sidetracked for a while after back surgery in the fall of 1995. Then Bono started losing his voice. Doctors told him to quit smoking or risk damaging his voice forever.

But the biggest problem with *Pop* was that their manager, Paul McGuinness, booked the tour before the album was finished. They were rushed to complete the album and were never satisfied with the outcome. As Larry put it, "If we had two or three more months to work, we would have had a very different record." The band may not have liked it that much, but the fans did. *Pop* reached number one in 29 countries, including the United Kingdom and the United States.

"*Pop* never had the chance to be properly finished. It is really the most expensive demo session in the history of music." -Bono

encore: a song played after a band ends the main part of a concert

The U2 PopMart tour featured a giant arc and a lemon, among other crazy props.

PopMart

One word could describe the PopMart tour—outrageous. And where better to kick off the flashy spectacle than Las Vegas? Problems followed the band on tour, however. They had trouble getting new songs to work live, and Bono frequently lost his voice. They also had technical difficulties with props. After their *encore*, the band returned to the stage in a giant, motorized lemon. But at several concerts the door didn't open.

4 Into the Heart

After the PopMart tour, U2 started writing new songs. For their next album, the band members left the glitz and glam behind. They returned to their rock 'n' roll roots. *All That You Can't Leave Behind* scored the band seven more Grammys between 2000 and 2001.

The stage production for the 2001 Elevation tour was also much simpler. A heart-shaped walkway surrounded the stage, allowing the band members to get closer to their fans.

After the terrorist attacks on September 11, 2001, U2 considered canceling the rest of the Elevation tour. Instead, they honored the heroic men and women of New York City's fire and police departments in their own special way. At a few shows, the band brought the heroes on stage during the closing song, "Walk On." The names of the victims of the terrorist attacks were also displayed on a video screen behind the stage.

U2 wows British fans at a 2001 concert.

I Can't Change the World, But I Can Change the World in Me

Bono's social activism began on a trip to Africa in 1985. There he and his wife, Ali, spent a month volunteering in an orphanage. They saw the poverty and starvation devastating Africa. Since then the members of U2 have played in many benefit concerts and supported various charities. In the late 1990s and early 2000s, Bono also became involved in politics. He has met with world leaders to persuade them to help the poor. He also helped start the organizations One Campaign and Product RED to fight poverty, as well as AIDS and other diseases.

I'm at a Place Called Vertigo

U2 came off the Elevation tour energized and ready to work on their next album. By the fall of 2003, a new album was complete. But as Larry put it, "The songs had a lot of things going for them, but they had no magic." So U2 had producer Steve Lillywhite rework all of the songs.

The extra time in the studio pushed back the release of the album until late 2004, but it paid off. According to The Edge and Paul McGuinness, *How to Dismantle an Atomic Bomb* was U2's best album to date. Fans and critics agreed. The album won eight Grammys, including Album of the Year.

U2 planned to promote *Atomic Bomb* with the Vertigo tour. But shortly before tickets went on sale, The Edge's daughter, Sian, was diagnosed with a serious illness. The band considered canceling the tour, but it was 7-year-old Sian who encouraged The Edge and the others to do it. By the time the Vertigo tour wrapped up in Hawaii on December 9, 2006, U2 had circled the globe once again.

U2 Trivia

In April 1998 the members of U2 appeared as themselves on the 200th episode of *The Simpsons.*

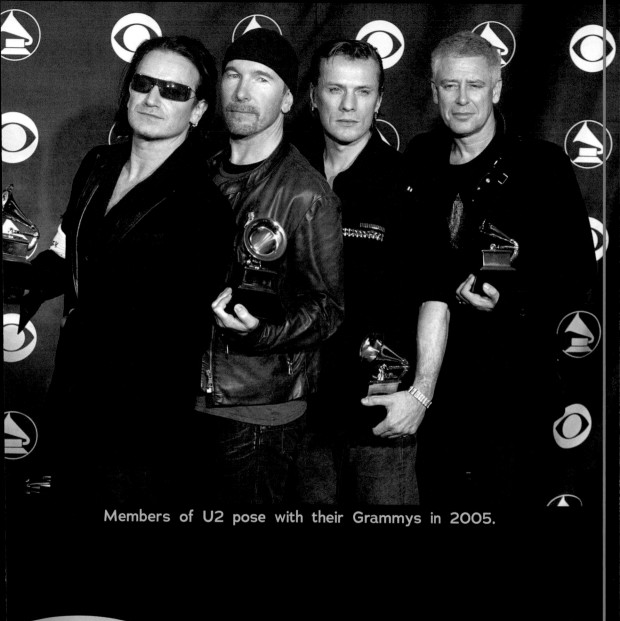

Members of U2 pose with their Grammys in 2005.

diagnose: to recognize a disease by signs and symptoms

Time Won't Take the Boy Out of This Man

In March 2009 U2 released *No Line on the Horizon*. It didn't sell as many as some of their other albums. But the 360° tour that followed was their most successful tour yet. More than 7.2 million tickets were sold.

The stage was surrounded by a massive four-legged structure called "The Claw." A large, expanding video screen showed shots of the band. The show also included a light show. A round stage, circular runway, and moving bridges let U2 get even closer to their fans. U2 also made sure that ticket prices remained affordable.

But trouble continued to torment the band. In May 2010 while rehearsing for the second North American leg of the tour, Bono suffered a serious back injury. He underwent emergency spinal surgery and had to go through weeks of follow-up therapy. As a result the tour was postponed until May 2011.

The Chance of a Lifetime

Bono often brings fans on stage during shows. Sometimes they simply dance with him, but others get to play a song with the band. In Nashville, Tennessee, in 2011, a blind man was pulled on stage to play "All I Want Is You." Bono let the lucky fan keep his guitar!

Fans in Poland form the Polish flag with colored paper during a 2009 U2 concert.

U2 was inducted into the Rock and Roll Hall of fame in 2005.

What Wε Havε Wε'rε Gonna Kεεp, Always

The members of U2 continue to reach new heights in their music and stage production. They continue to experiment and push their limits. Although they all get involved in side projects from time to time, the band is still each member's top priority. Still going strong since 1976, the musicians of U2 are some of the few legends of rock.

Chart Topper

With so many hits to choose from, pinpointing U2's most memorable song is no easy task. But "Where the Streets Have No Name" is definitely one of the band's most famous tunes. With The Edge's gritty guitar playing, Larry's energetic drumming, and Adam's sturdy bass, the song is instantly recognizable as a U2 staple. It didn't break the Top 10 when it was released in 1987, but decades later it still gets a lot of radio play. When played live no other song can get thousands of people on their feet faster than "Where the Streets Have No Name."

Songs of Innocence

U2 released their 13th studio album, *Songs of Innocence*, in October 2014. The album, which Bono described as "the blood, sweat, and tears of some Irish guys," was three and a half years in the making. A month before the release, U2 teamed up with Apple to give everyone a first look at the album—by dropping it into more than half a billion iTunes accounts for free. This innovative approach annoyed some people, but thrilled others. In the end the clever marketing strategy succeeded in reaching a new generation of fans who otherwise might never have listened to the album.

Glossary

benefit (BEN-uh-fit)—to be helped by something

chord (KORD)—a combination of musical notes played at the same time

diagnose (dy-ig-NOHS)—to recognize a disease by signs and symptoms

encore (AHN-kor)—a song played after a band ends the main part of a concert

famine (FA-muhn)—a serious shortage of food resulting in widespread hunger and death

Grammy Award (GRA-mee uh-WARD)—an award given at an annual music awards celebration that honors the year's best music

induct (in-DUHKT)—to formally admit someone into a position or place of honor

persona (pur-SO-nuh)—the image or personality that a person projects in public

rhythm (RIH-thum)—a regular beat in music, poetry, or dance

rockumentary (rok-yuh-MEN-tuh-ree)—a nonfiction movie or TV program about a rock band

Read More

Washburn, Kim. *Beyond the Music: the Bono Story*. Grand Rapids, Mich.: Zonderkidz, 2013.

Washburn, Kim. *Breaking Through by Grace: the Bono Story*. Zonderkids Biography. Grand Rapids, Mich.: Zonderkidz, 2010.

Winckelmann, Thom. *Bono: Rock Star & Humanitarian*. Essential Lives. Edina, Minn.: ABDO Publishing Company, 2010.

Internet Sites

FactHound offers a safe, fun way to find Internet sites related to this book. All of the sites on FactHound have been researched by our staff.

Here's all you do:

Visit *www.facthound.com*

Type in this code: 9781491418185

Super-cool stuff!

Check out projects, games and lots more at
www.capstonekids.com

Index

albums
    Achtung Baby, 16, 18
    All That You Can't Leave Behind, 22
    Boy, 10
    How to Dismantle an Atomic Bomb, 24
    Joshua Tree, The, 12
    No Line on the Horizon, 26
    October, 10
    Pop, 20
    Rattle and Hum, 14
    Unforgettable Fire, The, 12
    War, 10
    Zooropa, 18

Bono, 4, 6, 7, 8, 9, 10, 12, 14, 15, 16, 18, 19, 20, 21, 23, 26

Clayton, Adam, 6, 14, 16, 29

Edge, The, 6, 7, 8, 10, 11, 16, 17, 24, 29

Grammy Awards, 4, 12, 16, 22, 24

McGuinness, Paul, 17, 20, 24
Mullen, Larry Jr., 6, 10, 14, 16, 20, 24, 29

personas, 15, 18

tours
    360°, 26
    Elevation, 22, 24
    Joshua Tree, 15
    PopMart, 21, 22
    Vertigo, 24
    Zoo TV, 18, 19